Triangle Shirtwaist Factory Fire

Other titles in the *American Disasters* series:

Apollo 1 Tragedy
Fire in the Capsule
ISBN 0-7660-1787-7

Attack on America
The Day the Twin
Towers Collapsed
ISBN 0-7660-2118-1

The Challenger
Disaster
Tragic Space Flight
ISBN 0-7660-1222-0

Columbine High
School Shooting
Student Violence
ISBN 0-7660-1782-6

El Niño & La Niña
Deadly Weather
ISBN 0-7660-1551-3

The Exxon Valdez
Tragic Oil Spill
ISBN 0-7660-1058-9

The Hindenburg
Disaster
Doomed Airship
ISBN 0-7660-1554-8

Fire in Oakland,
California
Billion-Dollar Blaze
ISBN 0-7660-1220-4

Hurricane Andrew
Nature's Rage
ISBN 0-7660-1057-0

Jonestown Massacre
Tragic End of a Cult
ISBN 0-7660-1789-2

Love Canal
Toxic Waste Tragedy
ISBN 0-7660-1553-X

Mount St. Helens
Volcano
Violent Eruption
ISBN 0-7660-1552-1

The Oklahoma City
Bombing
Terror in the Heartland
ISBN 0-7660-1061-9

Pearl Harbor
Deadly Surprise Attack
ISBN 0-7660-1783-4

Polio Epidemic
Crippling Virus
Outbreak
ISBN 0-7660-1555-6

The Siege at Waco
Deadly Inferno
ISBN 0-7660-1218-2

The Titanic
Disaster at Sea
ISBN 0-7660-1557-2

Three Mile Island
Nuclear Disaster
ISBN 0-7660-1556-4

Triangle Shirtwaist
Factory Fire
Flames of
Labor Reform
ISBN 0-7660-1785-0

Tsunami
Monster Waves
ISBN 0-7660-1786-9

The World Trade
Center Bombing
Terror in the Towers
ISBN 0-7660-1056-2

Triangle Shirtwaist Factory Fire

Flames of Labor Reform

Michelle M. Houle

Enslow Publishers, Inc.

40 Industrial Road   PO Box 38
Box 398   Aldershot
Berkeley Heights, NJ 07922   Hants GU12 6BP
USA   UK

http://www.enslow.com

Library of Congress Cataloging-in-Publication Data

Houle, Michelle M.
    Triangle Shirtwaist Factory fire : flames of labor reform / Michelle M. Houle.
        p. cm. — (American disasters)
    Includes bibliographical references and index.
    Summary: Discusses the 1911 fire that killed 146 New York garment factory
workers, the conditions that led up to it, and some of the legislation that came
about to prevent the occurrence of similar disasters.
    ISBN 0-7660-1785-0
    1. Triangle Shirtwaist Company—Fire, 1911—Juvenile literature. 2. New York
(N.Y.)—History—1898-1951—Juvenile literature. 3. Clothing factories—New York
(State)—New York—Safety measures—History—20th century—Juvenile literature.
4. Labor laws and legislation—New York (State)—New York—History—20th century—Juvenile literature. [1. Triangle Shirtwaist Company—Fire, 1911. 2. Industrial
safety—History.] I. Title. II. Series.
F128.5 .H73   2002
974.7'1041—dc21

                                                        2001007667

Printed in the United States of America

10 9 8 7 6 5 4 3 2 1

To Our Readers:
We have done our best to make sure all Internet Addresses in this book were active and
appropriate when we went to press. However, the author and the publisher have no
control over and assume no liability for the material available on those Internet sites
or on other Web sites they may link to. Any comments or suggestions can be sent by e-
mail to comments@enslow.com or to the address on the back cover.

Illustration Credits: David Torsiello/Enslow Publishers, Inc., pp. 41, 42;
Enslow Publishers, Inc., pp. 13, 24; Franklin D. Roosevelt Library, pp. 1, 6, 11,
19, 26, 27, 28, 29, 31, 34, 38; Library of Congress, pp. 14, 33, 37, 40.

Cover Illustration: Courtesy of the New York City Board of Education.

Contents

*T*he Asch Building on the corner of Washington Place and
Greene Street in lower Manhattan was one of many buildings
where young immigrants would typically work six to seven
days a week at the beginning of the twentieth century.

CHAPTER 1

An Unforgettable Afternoon

Spring had begun happily in 1911 for the Hochfield family. Esther, only twenty years old, had just gotten engaged to be married. The family celebrated with a party that lasted until the early hours of the morning. The next day was a Monday, and Esther and her brother Max woke up late. They were happy but very tired. They decided to stay home from work to rest. They spent the day relaxing and cleaning up from the party.[1]

On Tuesday morning, Max and Esther Hochfield went back to work at the Triangle Shirtwaist Company factory. The factory was located on the top three floors of the ten-story Asch Building on the corner of Greene Street and Washington Place in New York City. The Hochfields worked there on the eighth floor.

When they arrived on that Tuesday morning, Esther and Max were told that their jobs had been given away because they had not come to work the day before. Luckily, every-one knew that the Hochfields were a fun-loving but hard-working family. Although they lost their jobs on the eighth floor, Max and Esther were given work on the ninth floor. Both of them were thankful to be employed because their family depended on their wages for survival.

A few days later, Max Hochfield was the first one waiting by the exit door after the bell rang to signal the end of the workday. It was 4:45 P.M. and it was a Saturday—payday. Max Hochfield was happy and excited. He and all the other Triangle workers had been looking forward to the end of the day when they would receive their weekly pay envelopes. Plus, the factory was usually closed on Sundays, so they had the next day off. With spring just around the corner, Max Hochfield was looking forward to a relaxing day away from the factory.

Smiling and joking with the forewoman, Max Hochfield eagerly tucked his pay into his pocket. He hoped that there would be a little bit of extra money to spend once he had given most of his pay to his family for their rent and food. Thinking about how he would spend his day off, Hochfield decided to wait for his sister outside. He knew that Esther would be talking to her friends while putting on her hat and coat in the dressing room. Esther Hochfield liked to talk with her friends about her upcoming marriage and Max knew she might take a while. He also knew that it always took a long time for the workers to exit the building since there was only one door open for them. On payday, the line moved even more slowly as the workers waited for their pay envelopes.

Making his way down the narrow staircase, Max

Hochfield slowed down as he neared the eighth floor. Going around a corner, he smelled smoke. Suddenly, he realized that the eighth floor was full of flames. Screams and cries of "Fire!" pierced the air.

Max Hochfield immediately thought of his sister who was still on the ninth floor, completely unaware of the fire raging below her. Turning around, he pushed back the people racing down around him trying to escape the flames. "Esther!" he cried. "I have to save my sister!" Seeing him try to go back up the stairs, a fireman stopped him.[2]

The fireman pushed Max Hochfield down the stairs and insisted that his sister would join him on the street below. Very reluctantly, Hochfield made his way down the smoky stairwell. On his way down, he helped some of his frightened co-workers escape the fire, but he never stopped worrying about Esther.

Max Hochfield would never see his sister alive again. One of the worst industrial fires in American history had just begun at the Triangle Shirtwaist Company factory.

CHAPTER 2

Unheard Warnings

There had been many danger signs before the fire at the Triangle Shirtwaist Factory on March 25, 1911. Just four months earlier, twenty-five workers had died in a similar fire in a factory in Newark, New Jersey, just across the river from Manhattan. Many of the people killed were young immigrant women, like the workers at the Triangle Factory. Those who had died had been burned to death or had jumped out of the factory windows in order to escape the flames.

Right after the factory fire in Newark, New York City Fire Chief Edward F. Croker issued a warning: "This city may have a fire as deadly as the one in Newark at any time," he said. "There are buildings in New York where the danger is every bit as great as in the building destroyed in Newark. A fire in the daytime would be accompanied by a terrible loss of life."[1]

At the time, there were very few laws that regulated safety measures for factories. Many factory owners, including the owners of the Triangle Shirtwaist Company factory, had only a small idea of the dangers lurking within their facilities. Following the Newark fire, investigations were planned to check the conditions of many of the factories in New York, including the Triangle factory. The owners of the factory, however, were not worried. They were breaking no laws and had listened to all the suggestions made by the fire department about fire safety regulations.

*T*he charred interior of one of the Asch Building's upper floors in the aftermath of the fire. Prior to the terrible blaze, the building had been considered fireproof.

The Triangle Shirtwaist Company factory had passed numerous inspections, including one only five months before the fire on March 25.[2] The workers at the Triangle factory made women's shirtwaists, a popular kind of blouse made of a thin, flimsy fabric that easily caught on fire. There had been minor fires in the factory in the Asch Building before, but the building was considered "fireproof." However, "fireproof" only meant that the building itself would not collapse if a fire occurred—it had nothing to do with the materials inside the building being resistant to fire.

Officially, the Asch Building and the Triangle Shirtwaist Company factory passed inspection with only "minor" problems. In addition to these, however, there were many fire hazards that the inspectors pointed out to the owners, Max Blank and Isaac Harris. For example, Blank and Harris did not offer fire drills to their workers. Also, there were no sprinklers in the Asch Building to put out any fires that might start. Since there were no laws requiring fire drills or sprinklers, Blank and Harris did not think that they were necessary.

A century ago, most city factories had serious fire safety problems. At the time, fire-fighting equipment could not reach higher than seven stories, but many factory buildings were much taller than that. Many did not have enough doors, staircases, or fire escapes to serve the number of people working in the factory. Most of the factories had doors that opened inward instead of out, which caused great confusion and difficulty when many people rushed to escape a room. Nearly all of the factories were overcrowded, and the equipment and materials were highly flammable. Disasters were inevitable.

The workers in the factories were often uneducated and poor. Because they needed money so badly, they had to accept unsafe working conditions. Women who worked in the garment industry were often exhausted, hungry, and unable to provide for their families. Workers knew that something had to be done to improve the factory system, but they desperately needed their jobs and the meager wages they provided in order to survive.

The shirtwaist style (as illustrated above) was very fashionable at the dawn of the twentieth century.

The nature of the work performed, the low wages, and the conditions of the factory had already prompted outrage among many factory workers by the time of the Triangle fire. From 1909–1910, a strike known as the "Uprising of the Twenty Thousand"

*T*his 1907 photo of the sewing room of a shirt factory in Troy, New York, depicts the cramped conditions that factory workers were typically forced to operate under at that time.

was staged to protest factory conditions. (A strike is when a group of people refuses to work in order to force the employer to meet the strikers' demands.) The International Ladies Garment Workers Union organized the strike, and it was supported by the Women's Trade Union League. The main concerns of the strike were mandatory overtime, too much work, low wages, and the process of "sweating," which meant that workers had to compete with each other for work and pay.[3]

The strike was a massive movement that spread throughout the entire women's garment industry. Nearly 40,000 workers went on strike. Many smaller factories immediately agreed to the union's demands because they could not afford to have their workers away for a long period of time. Unfortunately, the larger companies did not always agree to the demands of the union. They could afford to close their factories until they could hire strike-breakers to work in the place of the union workers. The Triangle Shirtwaist Company was one of these companies.

The great strike actually began in 1909 at the Triangle Shirtwaist Company factory, where the workers—mostly young women and girls—had walked off the job together in protest. The strike went on for many months and there were many protests throughout the city. Sometimes striking workers were arrested while protesting the conditions of the factories. Often, teenage girls who protested were arrested because they had no way of defending themselves against the thugs hired by the factories to stop their protests. With the help of some rich benefactors like Anne Morgan (the daughter of banker J. P. Morgan), the International Ladies Garment Workers Union helped these girls to continue their fight against the factory owners.

The great strike lasted from November 1909 to February 1910. By February, 354 firms had come to some sort of agreement with the union. However, thirteen firms with a total of 1,100 workers did not settle with the union. The Triangle Shirtwaist Company was one of these thirteen firms.[4] If the company had agreed to the contract, no workers would have been in the Triangle Shirtwaist Company factory at 4:45 P.M. on March 25, 1911, because the union agreement required a half-day's work on Saturday.[5]

Despite the efforts of the striking workers, wages remained low and the working conditions in the Triangle factory did not improve. Few safety measures were ever taken to protect the workers.

CHAPTER 3

FIRE!

At 4:45 P.M. on Saturday, March 25, 1911, the bell rang, signaling the end of the workday. It was the end of another long week for the workers at the Triangle Shirtwaist Factory on the eighth, ninth, and tenth floors of the Asch Building. Around the four-hundred-square-foot room, chairs scratched against the floor as the workers rose wearily from their tables.

Most of the workers were young immigrant women from Italy or Eastern Europe. They earned between $9 and $16 a week. This was just enough to pay the rent for a small apartment in a rundown neighborhood where the people were poor but hardworking. Many of them were religious Jews who were going against their faith by working on a Saturday. All of them were poor but working hard to improve their lot in life. The end of the workday was a moment of pleasure for everyone on Saturday because they always received their weekly pay at the end of the day on Saturdays and there was no work on Sundays.

Though they were tired, the workers were looking forward to a full meal that night in celebration of the money they had worked so hard to earn. Then they would have a day of rest on Sunday with their families and friends.

As the workers were lining up on the eighth floor, chatting happily about their plans for their day off on Sunday, Eva Harris, a sister of one of the company's owners, smelled smoke. She ran to the production manager, Samuel Bernstein, who turned to see flames coming out from one of the bins beneath the tables in the center of the room.[1] With a cry, Samuel Bernstein rushed to the table where some workers tried to put out the fire with water.

No one knows exactly what started the fire that afternoon. Someone may have accidentally flicked a match into one of the bins beneath the tables after lighting a cigarette. These bins were filled with scraps of cloth that caught fire very easily. The scraps were sold to a dealer named Louis Levy who removed them five or six times a year. The last time he removed the scraps was January 15, three months earlier. On March 25, the bins were full of fabric and thin paper.[2]

Because there were scraps of fabric underneath the tables and flimsy patterns hanging from wires all over the room, the fire spread very quickly. Samuel Bernstein worked with some of the other men to put out the fire. The men threw buckets of water on the fire. Seeing that this was not working, they grew nervous. They tried to use a hose, but it did not work. There was no water pressure and the hose was rotted in some places. Desperately, the men continued to work to put out the fire, despite the smoke and heat. But it was useless. Soon the fire was raging out of control and the whole floor was covered in flames.

The danger was soon clear to everyone on the eighth floor. The workers realized that they needed to escape the deadly flames. There was nothing they could do to save the shirtwaists they had worked so hard to produce. They had to save themselves no matter how frightened they were.

*C*ity firefighters were quick to respond to the fire at the Triangle Shirtwaist Factory on March 25, 1911.

In the panic and the smoke, Dinah Lifschitz ran to the office where there was a telephone and a telautograph—a machine for transmitting hand-written messages.[3] Though she was terrified and the smoke was getting thicker by the minute, Lifschitz tried to use the telautograph but nothing seemed to work correctly. Finally, she was able to reach someone in the executive office on the tenth floor by telephone. After warning the people on the tenth floor, she tried to call the ninth floor, but she could not get through. It seemed that the switchboard was not working and Lifschitz soon gave up, realizing that she had to leave in order to survive the fire.

While Lifschitz was on the telephone, the chaos was growing wilder. Screams filled the air as hysterical people rushed toward the stairway doors. Unfortunately, the doors appeared to be locked. Frightened women and girls pushed and pulled at the doors, but they would not open.

Finally, someone was able to open one of the stairway doors on the eighth floor. Terrified women and girls spilled through and down the narrow stairs to the street below, their hair flying wildly and their clothing burned and grayed by the smoke.

CHAPTER 4

The Fire Spreads

On Saturday, March 25, 1911, the tenth floor office at the Triangle Shirtwaist Factory was busier than usual because it was payday. Also, two children, Henrietta and Mildred Blank, had come to the office to meet their father, Max Blank, one of the factory's co-owners. They were to go shopping when he had finished his work. Many people were milling about in the office, busy but happy at the end of another long week.

Another reason the office had been particularly hectic that day was because the regular factory switchboard operator was ill. A woman named Mary Alter had taken over her duties. Alter was a typist who worked in the offices on the tenth floor of the Asch Building with about seventy other people. She was not used to working the switchboard that connected the floors of the building together by telephone. She answered the phone at 4:45 that afternoon and listened as a hysterical Dinah Lifschitz gave the fire alarm. Alter herself became desperately worried. She rushed to tell the news to the owners of the factory, who were both working in their offices that afternoon. Then she went to warn her father, a watchman on the tenth floor.

Unfortunately, as Mary Alter moved about the office to warn Max Blank, Isaac Harris, and her father, no one was left to work the switchboard. On the eighth floor, Dinah Lifschitz was frantically trying to call the ninth floor in order to warn them, but she was unable to make the call because no one was at the switchboard to connect her. As people began to evacuate the eighth and tenth floors, no one on the ninth floor had any idea that a fire was raging below.

Most of the people on the tenth floor could not fit into the elevators, and the stairs were already full of smoke. The only way they could escape was to climb to the roof and then climb over to the roof of the New York University building next door. This is how Max Blank escaped the fire with his children Henrietta and Mildred. They cried and clutched at their father in fear. Law students from the university building had heard the sounds of the fire engines and had climbed to the roof in order to rescue the frightened people next door. The Asch Building was about twelve feet lower than the University building, so students lowered a ladder across to help factory workers escape.[1]

The workers on the tenth floor were luckier than some of the others and nearly all escaped the fire. Only one person from the tenth floor was killed. Her name was

Clotilda Terdanova. She had become so frightened that she thought there was no way she would ever be able to survive the fire so she jumped out of a window before anyone could stop her. Like Esther Hochfield, Terdanova was engaged to be married and her wedding was supposed to be only a month after the fire.[2]

On the ninth floor, the workers were not as lucky as those on the eighth and tenth floors. There were nearly 250 people working on the ninth floor that day and they were packed in very closely at tables that ran the entire length of the floor. Many of these people never made it out of the building alive.

There were three exits from the main room on the ninth floor—one on the Greene Street side, one on the Washington Place side, and a fire escape that ended on the second floor above an enclosed courtyard. The doors on the ninth floor were usually locked during the day because the factory owners wanted to keep track of the workers. Everyone always left at the end of the day through the one exit on the Greene Street side of the building.[3] Most of the workers did not know about the fire escape because it was behind a set of metal shutters. So, despite the fact that there were three exits, only one was actually available to the workers.

Because no one on the ninth floor knew about the fire, the workday ended on that Saturday as it usually did. The forewoman rang the bell, and the workers stopped sewing at their machines. Most of the workers were young women and when they heard the bell, they hurried to the

FLOOR PLAN OF THE
TRIANGLE SHIRTWAIST FACTORY

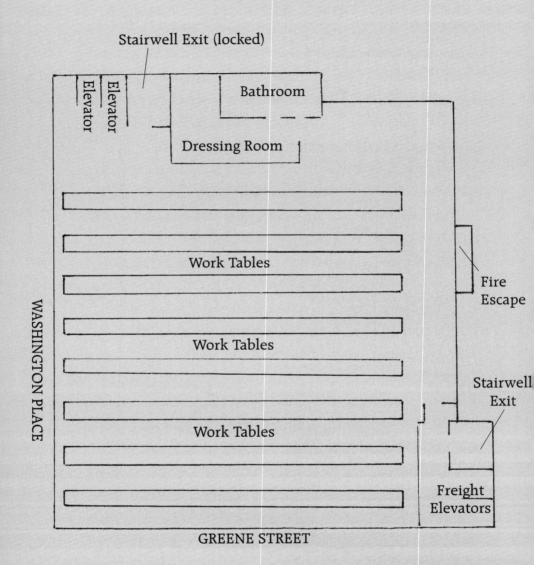

Stairwell Exit (locked)

Elevator
Elevator
Elevator

Bathroom

Dressing Room

WASHINGTON PLACE

Work Tables

Work Tables

Work Tables

Fire
Escape

Stairwell
Exit

Freight
Elevators

GREENE STREET

This floor plan shows the layout of the ninth floor of the
Asch Building. There were eight long work tables which
held a total of 240 sewing machines. Chairs and work
baskets blocked the aisles, forcing many workers to
climb over the tables to escape.

dressing room on the Washington Place side of the room to put on their coats and freshen up before leaving for the day. While they were in the dressing room, they began to sing happily, excited to receive their pay envelopes and looking forward to a restful Sunday. Because they were singing, they did not hear the cries coming from the floor below them where the fire had begun. When the happy workers exited the dressing room, they saw the flames from the eighth floor and their songs turned into screams of fright.

The young women were terrified and they did not know which way to run. The flames had begun to spread throughout the room and it was very hot and smoky. No one could see very well and it seemed that no one could move without her skirt or hair catching fire. Most of the young women had gone into the dressing room near the exit door on the Washington Place side of the room and although this door was the closest exit for many of the workers, it would not open.

The room on the ninth floor had 240 sewing machines crammed together in it, and it was very difficult to get from one end of the room to the other because there were long tables covering the entire floor. The room was soon entirely full of flames and few of the young women were able to climb over the tables and machines to the open Greene Street door.

One of the few women who was able to escape from the ninth floor was named Anna Gullo. She worked at the Triangle Factory with her sister Mary. At first, she had

*T*he Asch Building's ninth-floor fire escape was behind these two large metal shutters. Many of the workers trapped on the ninth floor on the day of the fire did not even know the fire escape was there.

tried to open the Washington Place door but it seemed to be locked. Terrified, she tried to help fight the fire but the water she threw only seemed to make the flames leap higher. Crying for her sister, Anna Gullo made her way to the windows near the locked door. Though she considered jumping to avoid the flames, she was frightened by the height. Somewhere in the confusion, she was hit by a bucket of water, soaking her to the skin. This accident may have saved her life. Pulling her wet, woolen skirt over her head, Anna dove through the flames and went down the stairs on the Greene Street side of the building. By the time she reached the street, her hair and clothing were burned. Anna never saw her sister Mary alive again.[4]

Only a few young women knew about the fire escape behind the metal shutters at the back of the room. Jumping over flames, these women pulled back the shutters and climbed out of the inferno. Unfortunately, the fire escape was not well made and it collapsed after only a few people had climbed down. Fewer than twenty people were saved by using the fire escape.[5] Some people were still able to climb to the roof and escape along with the workers from the tenth floor by climbing across to the New York University building next door.

Once the fire escape had collapsed and the workers realized that the Washington Place doors would not open, their only hope was the elevators next to the Washington Place staircase. There were two elevators on the Washington Place side of the room and they were only supposed to fit fifteen passengers each. An operator ran each elevator and they did not work automatically. On the day of the fire, the elevators carried nearly thirty screaming people during each trip. The elevator operators probably made about eight trips each, and they saved hundreds of people. Sadly, as the women on the ninth floor backed away from the flames, some of them fell or jumped into

The twisted remains of the fire escape ladder in the wake of the deadly blaze on March 25, 1911.

The hole at the bottom of the Asch Building's ninth-floor fire escape, which collapsed on the day of the fire. Less than twenty people were able to successfully use it to escape.

the elevator shaft. Most of these women died and the weight of their bodies eventually kept the elevators from rising again to save more people.

Cut off from the one open door and unable to use either the elevators or the fire escape, the women on the ninth floor felt doomed. The flames were reaching higher, the room was getting hotter, and the smoke was so thick that everyone was coughing, unable to breathe. Many of the workers were terrified and jumped out of the windows to avoid being burned alive. Though they may have thought that this would save their lives, the fall from the ninth floor was fatal. Firefighters stretched out large nets and tried to catch the falling workers, their hair streaming behind them. The women, however, plunged right through the nets, sometimes even crashing through the sidewalk into the basement below. More than sixty people died by falling or jumping from the upper stories of the building.

*F*irefighters try to douse the flames raging on the upper floors of the Asch Building on March 25, 1911.

CHAPTER 5

Alarm Bells in the City

The day of the Triangle fire started out calmly. Spring was peaking through the cold and winter seemed to be drawing to a comfortable close. Near the factory, people were strolling through Washington Square Park and students were studying at New York University. The Triangle Shirtwaist Factory fire changed the lives of all of these people, whether or not they knew anyone who worked in the factory. Many people responded to the crisis with true bravery. Were it not for these heroes, many more people might have died on that fateful day.

One of the first people outside the building to notice the fire at the Triangle Shirtwaist Factory was a reporter named William Gunn Shepherd. Shepherd worked for the United Press and was the only reporter at the scene of the tragedy. While flames flickered out the broken windows of the Asch Building, Shepherd raced to a store and dictated the story of the fire to his editor over the telephone. "Thud—dead. Thud—dead," he wrote as he saw the bodies

*T*he bodies of women who leaped to their deaths to escape the fire lie covered in front of the Asch Building on March 25, 1911.

of the workers fall from the upper floors of the Asch Building.[1] Shepherd's words appeared in newspapers across America later that day, delivering the tragic news.

Dr. D. C. Winterbottom was a coroner for the city. (A coroner is a doctor who investigates unnatural deaths.) He lived on the south side of Washington Square, just down the street from the factory. That Saturday afternoon, he was looking out his window when he saw people rushing towards the Asch Building. Grabbing his medical bag, he raced after them. When he got to the Asch Building, he was shocked. He ran to telephone for ambulances to be sent to the scene. After he made this phone call, Dr. Winterbottom immediately began to help the victims.

One of the first policeman at the scene was Patrolman James P. Meehan, who was riding his horse through Washington Square Park when the fire started. He heard an explosion as the force of the fire blew out one of the windows on the eighth floor of the Asch Building. Dismounting his horse, he ran into the building and climbed eight flights of stairs until he reached a wave of frightened women and girls running away from the fire. He helped them as best he could, carrying out one girl who had fainted. Then Patrolman Meehan continued to help firefighters battle the inferno.[2]

The first alarm was sounded at 4:45 P.M. that Saturday afternoon. Firefighters arrived at the scene as quickly as they could. Although their hoses were ready, the firefighters' ladders only reached the seventh floor and even their high-pressure hoses could not reach the top floors of the building. When the firefighters spread their nets to try to save the falling workers, the victims plunged right through, knocking their would-be rescuers right off their feet.

Help was on the way, but the workers were cut off from the exits almost immediately after the start of the fire. It took only three minutes for the fire to spread from the eighth floor to the ninth and tenth floors.[3] Within

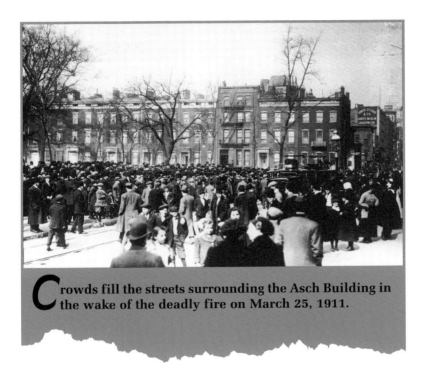

*C*rowds fill the streets surrounding the Asch Building in the wake of the deadly fire on March 25, 1911.

minutes, frightened workers began to jump or fall from the windows of the eighth, ninth, and tenth floors of the Asch Building. Only twelve minutes after the fire had started on the eighth floor, the last young woman jumped from the ninth floor, her hair and skirt on fire and smoke streaming behind her. All told, sixty-two people had fallen from the factory windows. Within twenty minutes of the first alarm, the fire was under control. Just ten minutes later, the fire was almost extinguished. Within that short half hour, 146 people either burned to death or were killed by falling from the windows of the Asch Building.

After the tragedy, the city began to grieve. Even as the alarm bells were ringing, word spread quickly throughout the city. By nightfall, crowds had gathered around the Asch Building. Many of the people were relatives of Triangle workers searching for their loved ones. Others were there to show their support for the victims. As with many tragedies, however, there were some people who came just to stare at the building in gory fascination. The crowd was huge and policeman were called upon to keep the people away from the building.

Grief-stricken family members suffered the grim task of having to identify the remains of loved ones who had lost their lives in the Triangle Shirtwaist Factory fire.

Ambulances took the injured to hospitals throughout the city. Wagons took the corpses to a makeshift morgue on a pier on the east side of Manhattan. Soon the line of mourners stretched for blocks as families searched for their sons and daughters, husbands and wives, mothers and fathers. There were some happy, joyful reunions, but often, cries of grief rang out as a lost loved one was recognized by a special piece of jewelry or an article of clothing. In the end, seven out of the 146 bodies were unidentified.

CHAPTER 6

Can There Be Justice?

New Yorkers were angry that so many people—most of them young immigrant women—had died in a fire that could have been avoided. There were protests throughout the city and many people were ready to pass judgment on those they thought were responsible for the fire. Many families were left with nothing when their sole providers died in the fire. Charities such as the Red Cross raised money from all corners of the world to help the victims and their families.

The tragedy made people realize that something needed to be done to protect workers. Anne Morgan, a rich New York socialite, rented the Metropolitan Opera House on April 2 so that the Women's Trade Union League could hold a large meeting. There, they would decide what could be done to avoid any future accidents.

That afternoon, Rose Schneiderman spoke before the assembly. Schneiderman was a former garment worker and union leader who later was very involved in New

*T*he front page of the *New York World* as it appeared on March 26, 1911, the day after the tragic fire.

Deal politics. (The New Deal was a program begun in the 1930s by President Franklin D. Roosevelt. It was designed to promote economic recovery and social reform.) Before the huge crowd a the Opera House, she offered this emotional speech:

> I would be a traitor to those poor burned bodies if I were to come here to talk good fellowship. We have tried you good

*F*irst Lady Eleanor Roosevelt and Rose Schneiderman (seated) address the Women's Trade Union League on May 5, 1936. Schneiderman became a strong voice for labor reforms in the wake of the fire.

people of the public—and we have found you wanting. The old Inquisition had its rack and its thumbscrews and its instruments of torture with iron teeth. We know what these things are today: the iron teeth are our necessities, the thumbscrews are the high-powered and swift machinery close to which we must work, and the rack is here in the firetrap structures that will destroy us the minute they catch on fire.

This is not the first time girls have been burned alive in the city. Every week I must learn of the untimely death of one of my sister workers. Every year thousands of us are maimed. The life of men and women is so cheap and property is so sacred! There are so many of us for one job, it matters little if 140-odd are burned to death.

We have tried you, citizens! We are trying you now and you have a couple of dollars for the sorrowing mothers and brothers and sisters by way of a charity gift. But every time the workers come out in the only way they know to protest against conditions which are unbearable, the strong hand of the law is allowed to press down heavily upon us.

Public officials have only words of warning to us—warning that we must be intensely orderly and must be intensely peaceable, and they have the workhouse just back of all their warnings. The strong hand of the law beats us back when we rise—back into the conditions that make life unbearable.

I can't talk fellowship to you who are gathered here. Too much blood has been spilled. I know from experience it is up to the working people to save themselves. And the only way is through a strong working-class movement.[1]

At the Metropolitan Opera House meeting, participants created the Factory Investigating Commission, which became a legal entity in June. The Commission was led by Robert Wagner and Al Smith. Smith would later go on to serve four terms as Governor of the state of New York.

The Factory Investigating Commission combined the forces of the Women's Trade Union League with other activists in order to investigate the state of factories throughout the city. Despite the sorrows caused by the fire, the tragedy at the Triangle Shirtwaist Company factory ultimately helped to usher in an era of reform when unions grew in size and power and laws were passed to help protect workers and safeguard their rights.

The meeting at the Metropolitan Opera House was just one indication of the city's grief. Two days later on April 5, cries rose up again in New York City as a funeral procession made its way from Washington Square up Fifth Avenue in the rain. The funeral was held in honor of the seven unidentified victims of the fire. More than 120,000 people marched that day through the great arch at Washington Square in a mass outpouring of sorrow. It is estimated that another 280,000 watched the parade in sadness, showing their support to the workers and their families. Known now for her speech at the Opera House,

*P*olitical drawings such as Glintenkamp's *Girls Wanted*, above, depicted the perceived greed and heartlessness of factory owners. Such drawings were a reflection of the city's mood in the wake of the fire.

Rose Schneiderman led the army of black-clad mourners past onlookers leaning out of buildings just as high and unsafe as the Asch Building. As she passed, Schneiderman was sickened by the thought that these people could perish just as easily as the workers in the Triangle Factory.[2] Their only hope was that reform would come before another tragedy occurred.

In mid-April, charges were brought against Max Blank and Isaac Harris, the owners of the Triangle Shirtwaist Company, in an attempt to bring justice to the victims of the fire and their relatives. The trial began in early December 1911.

Blank and Harris could not be charged with murder because there was no evidence that they intentionally caused harm to any of the victims. However, they might have violated a state labor law that required all doors to be unlocked during working hours. This violation was a misdemeanor, but if someone had died as a result of this violation, then Blank and Harris could be convicted of manslaughter. This was the law the courts used to try the owners of the Triangle Factory.

The main arguments at the trial revolved around whether the door was locked on the ninth floor on the Washington Place side, whether Blank and Harris knew and intended for the door to be locked, and whether anyone died specifically because of their actions. The trial lasted three weeks. While there seemed to be evidence to show that the door was indeed locked, there were many questions as to

*T*his memorial stone stands in Brooklyn's Cemetery of the Evergreens to commemorate the seven unidentified victims who died in the Triangle Shirtwaist Factory fire.

how the door had come to be locked and whether or not Blank and Harris had meant for the door to be locked. The jury had to acquit Blank and Harris because they did not have enough convincing evidence to show that Blank and Harris had locked the doors or that they were the cause of the deaths of the factory workers. It was a case of "reasonable doubt," but many people continued to feel that justice had not been done.[3]

In October 1911, laws were passed to establish the Bureau of Fire Prevention and to expand the responsibilities

*T*he inscription placed upon the Evergreens Cemetery monument that was erected for the seven unidentified victims of the fire.

of the Fire Commissioner. The Factory Investigating Commission was also working tirelessly during this time to pass laws providing safer conditions for workers in factories. Before 1914, dozens of laws were passed as a result of the efforts of organizations founded after the Triangle Factory fire. These laws regulated working hours, fire safety, child labor laws, and general working conditions.

The Triangle Shirtwaist Company fire was the horrific climax of years of hard labor and difficult conditions for American workers. No one could forget the sound and sight of the young women falling from the flaming Asch Building. After the fire, many steps were taken to prevent future tragedies. The workers at the Triangle Shirtwaist Factory died tragically. But even today they are remembered, and because of new laws, their deaths were not in vain.

Other Fires in the United States

DATE	PLACE	OUTCOME
October 8, 1871	Peshtigo, WI	More than 1,100 dead and 2 billion trees burned in forest fire.
October 8, 1871	Chicago, IL	250 dead; 17,450 buildings burned.
December 5, 1876	Brooklyn, NY	More than 300 dead in theater fire.
September 1, 1894	Minnesota	480 dead and six towns destroyed in forest fire.
December 30, 1903	Chicago, IL	602 dead at Iroquois Theatre.
June 15, 1904	New York, NY	1,030 dead in excursion boat fire on the East River.
March 4, 1908	Collingwood, OH	175 children dead in schoolhouse fire.
April 21, 1930	Columbus, OH	320 inmates dead at Ohio State Penitentiary.
March 18, 1937	New London, TX	294 dead in schoolhouse explosion and fire.
November 28, 1942	Boston, MA	491 dead at Coconut Grove nightclub.
July 6, 1944	Hartford, CT	168 dead in fire and ensuing stampede in the main tent of Ringling Brothers Circus.
December 7, 1946	Atlanta, GA	119 dead at Winecoff Hotel.
April 16, 1947	Texas City, TX	516 dead from explosion and fire.
December 1, 1958	Chicago, IL	95 dead at private school.
June 30, 1974	Port Chester, NY	24 dead in discotheque fire.
May 28, 1977	Southgate, KY	167 dead at Beverly Hills Supper Club.
November 21, 1980	Las Vegas, NV	84 dead at MGM Grand Hotel.
September 4, 1982	Los Angeles, CA	24 dead in apartment fire.
March 25, 1990	New York, NY	87 dead at Happy Land Social Club.
October 20, 1991	Oakland, CA	26 dead; three thousand homes destroyed; five thousand people left homeless; total damages estimated at $1.5 billion.

Chapter 1: An Unforgettable Afternoon

1. Leon Stein, *The Triangle Fire* (Ithaca, N.Y.: Cornell University Press, 2001), p. 54.

2. Ibid.

Chapter 2: Unheard Warnings

1. Leon Stein, *The Triangle Fire* (Ithaca, N.Y.: Cornell University Press, 2001), p. 27.

2. Ibid., p. 28.

3. John F. McClymer, *The Triangle Strike and Fire* (New York: Harcourt Brace College Publishers, 1998), p. 108.

4. Ibid., p. 24.

5. Ibid., p. 6.

Chapter 3: FIRE!

1. Leon Stein, *The Triangle Fire* (Ithaca, N.Y.: Cornell University Press, 2001), p. 34.

2. Ibid., p. 33.

3. Ibid., p. 37.

Chapter 4: The Fire Spreads

1. Paul Rosa, "The Triangle Shirtwaist Fire," *The History Buff*, n.d., <http://www.historybuff.com/library/refshirtwaist.html> (April 19, 2002).

2. Leon Stein, *The Triangle Fire* (Ithaca, N.Y.: Cornell University Press, 2001), p. 47.

3. Phillip S. Foner, *Women and the American Labor Movement* (New York: The Free Press, 1979), p. 359.

4. John F. McClymer, *The Triangle Strike and Fire* (New York: Harcourt Brace College Publishers, 1998), p. 135.

5. Stein, pp. 55–56.

Chapter 5: Alarm Bells in the City

1. Leon Stein, *The Triangle Fire* (Ithaca, N.Y.: Cornell University Press, 2001), p. 19.

2. Stein, pp. 12–15; John F. McClymer, *The Triangle Strike and Fire* (New York: Harcourt Brace College Publishers, 1998), p. 136.

3. McClymer, p. 135.

Chapter 6: Can There Be Justice?

1. John F. McClymer, *The Triangle Strike and Fire* (New York: Harcourt Brace College Publishers, 1998), pp. 144–145.

2. Ibid., pp. 102–104.

3. "147 Dead, Nobody Guilty," *Literary Digest*, January 6, 1912, <http://www.ilr.cornell.edu/trianglefire/texts/newspaper/ld_010612.html> (April 19, 2002).

coroner—A medical official who investigates unnatural deaths.

fellowship—A state of friendship or companionship.

fire escape—A metal ladder or stairway attached to the outside of a building designed to allow escape in case of a fire.

fireproof—resistant to fire.

hazard—A source of risk or danger.

morgue—A place where dead bodies are kept until they are identified or claimed by relatives.

mourner—Someone who expresses sadness over the death of another person.

New Deal—The program begun in the 1930s by President Franklin D. Roosevelt that was designed to promote economic recovery and social reform.

protest—A public demonstration by a group of people designed to voice objections to a set of conditions.

reform—To improve or change something for the better.

shirtwaist—A popular kind of blouse in the early 1900s made of a thin, flimsy fabric.

strike—When a group of people refuse to work in order to force their employer to meet their demands.

strikebreaker—A person who is hired to replace a striking worker.

"sweating"—A process whereby workers compete with each other for work and wages.

switchboard—A panel with electric switches that connect circuits (as in a telephone exchange).

telautograph—A machine used for transmitting hand-written messages.

union—An organization of individual workers whose purpose is to increase workers' benefits and labor conditions.

Further Reading

De Angelis, Gina. *The Triangle Shirtwaist Company Fire of 1911.* Broomall, Pa.: Chelsea, 2000.

Goldin, Barbara Diamond. *Fire! The Beginnings of the Labor Movement.* New York: Viking, 1992.

Littlefield, Holly. *Fire at the Triangle Factory.* Minneapolis, Minn.: Carolrhoda Books, 1996.

McClymer, John F. *The Triangle Strike and Fire.* New York: Harcourt Brace College Publishers, 1998.

Sherrow, Victoria. *The Triangle Factory Fire.* Brookfield, Conn.: Millbrook Press, 1995.

Stein, Leon. *The Triangle Fire.* Ithaca, N.Y.: Cornell University Press, 2001.

Internet Addresses

The Triangle Factory Fire
http://www.ilr.cornell.edu/trianglefire

Reform and the Triangle Shirtwaist Company Fire
http://www.tcr.org/triangle.html

Triangle Shirtwaist Fire—The Encyclopedia of New York City
http://www.yale.edu/yup/ENYC/triangle_shirtwaist.html

Rose Freedman: Last Survivor of the Triangle Factory Fire
http://radio.cbc.ca/programs/thismorning/sites/people/triangle_010225.html

Index